The Future of the United States:
It is Written in the Stars

BY
SUSIE COX

Printed in the United States of America

First Printing, 2020

ISBN-13: 978-1-947637-13-9 print edition
ISBN-13: 978-1-947637-14-6 ebook edition

Waterside Productions
2055 Oxford Ave
Cardiff, CA 92007
www.waterside.com

*This book is dedicated to **We the People**, you and me,
who will change the world.*

*Special thanks to my dear friend, Tom Whatley, who has
helped me with my writing for decades.*

Table of Contents

Notes from the Author

Humanity is experiencing unprecedented current events. We are in need of some serious decision making. The world is on almost total lockdown while fighting a raging pandemic. Millions of people are suddenly out of work and we have economic devastation not seen since the Great Depression. Some say it's worse. On top of that, we are experiencing demonstrations and racial riots in the streets while we prepare for a very heated presidential election. As I write this, fires are engulfing California and hurricanes are bombarding the Gulf of Mexico. Help!

Recently I was talking with a friend about the craziness happening in the world and we brought up the chart of the US. Since the orbit of Pluto is 249 years and the US is almost 245 years old, I thought that this would be a good time to look at that transit. Pluto is the planet of transformation and this will be of immense importance for the country.

To get to know the signature of Pluto better, we're going to take a stroll through recent history and see what events synchronized with the movement of Pluto since the birth of the US on July 4, 1776. That will give us a better blueprint of what to expect with the most crucial cycle of all, the Pluto Return.

We're also going to take a longer trip through history and get to know the Astrological Ages. We are currently ending the Age of Pisces and will be entering the Age of Aquarius and we are feeling the birth pains of that transition now in the world with these current difficult events. So, we'll be traveling back through space and time and will end up looking into the future. We'll be using Pluto as our muse, so it's going to be an exciting ride.

PART ONE:
The Astrology Chart for the USA

Everybody is confused now and we're looking for answers. As an astrologer, when things get weird, I cast a chart and see what's happening. It always soothes me because I can see a bigger picture, and now is one of those times. A new perspective will offer helpful information that will absolutely empower the human collective spirit... when it is needed the most.

So, what is this ancient language called Astrology? An astrology chart is the picture of the solar system at any moment in time. When a person or a country is born, if you could go outside and take a photo of the planets in the sky, freeze frame it and put it down on paper, that's a birth chart. The chart defines a purpose of a birth and points to challenges as well as talents and gifts. I have found it as one of the best tools known for self-understanding, which is why it's been around for so long. Since the US had a beginning or a birth, it therefore has a birth chart, which we will examine, and I promise you will understand. So, who is the US? What are its challenges or Karma? What are its talents and contributions to the world?

The United States was born on July 4th, 1776 at 5:10 p.m., in Philadelphia, PA. The Sun is in the sign of Cancer. The Sun sign always represents the inner essence of the subject. Cancer is interested in helping people with a nurturing, family-oriented and caring style. We all know the words inscribed on the Statue of Liberty. It's a poem by Emma Lazarus, *"Give me your tired, your poor, your huddled masses yearning to breathe free..."*

The next important points in every chart are the Moon and Rising Sign. The Moon describes the emotional state and in the US chart is the pulse of society. The Rising Sign is the outside personality or how we are perceived by the world.

The Cancer Sun is the mother energy who nurtures everyone. The US was built on diversity, bringing immigrants together in the melting pot called America. The goal of the Cancer Sun in the US chart is to include everyone.

The Moon is in the inventive sign of Aquarius. The Moon represents the pulse of society. Aquarius is considered the inventor of all the signs of the Zodiac and is always interested in what's new and modern. Equality and independence are also keywords for Aquarius as are computers, medical technology and the future. This Moon in Aquarius perfectly describes the social pulse of the United States, the new kid on the block.

The Rising Sign is in outspoken Sagittarius. Sagittarius is the sign of humanitarian projects, philosophy, international pursuits with an adventurous and enthusiastic spirit. The US was built on the philosophy of the melting pot. Remember, that except for the Indigenous Americans, all citizens in the US are descendants from immigrants. All of us.

Now we're going to look at the chart of the United States. This chart is a picture of the solar system on July 4, 1776 in Philadelphia. The planets in all charts are portrayed as symbols. Each planet occupies a house. There are 12 houses starting at the rising sign with the 1st house, then we move to the 2nd house counterclockwise all the way to the 12th house. Each house describes a different part of life. The symbol sheet shows the glyphs for the planets and signs and keywords for each house.

USA Signing Declaration
Natal Chart
Jul 4 1776 NS, Thu
5:10 pm LMT +5:00:39
Philadelphia, PA
39°N57'08" 075°W09'51"
Geocentric
Tropical
Equal
True Node

THE PLANETS AND THEIR QUALITIES

The planets represent the basic characters or archetypes in the chart. Mars is action and drive, while Venus is about love. All the planets have a different job to do to contribute the whole picture or chart.

Planets

☉   **Sun** — Inner essence, Core expression or Ego

☽   **Moon** — Emotions, Feelings or Holding on

☿   **Mercury** — Mentality, Communication or Cunning

♀   **Venus** — Love, Beauty or Vanity

♂   **Mars** — Action, Drive or Aggression

♃   **Jupiter** — Abundance, Adventure or Indulgence

♄   **Saturn** — Responsibility, Authority or Limitations

♅   **Uranus** — Freedom, Individuality or Revolution

♆   **Neptune** — Compassion, Inspiration or Fears

♇   **Pluto** — Power, Strength or Control

THE SIGNS AND THEIR PERSONALITIES

Other important parts of the chart are the Signs of the Zodiac. The signs are the personalities in Astrology that start with Aries and end with Pisces.

The signs have different personalities, idiosyncrasies and tendencies.

Signs

♈ **Aries** – Courageous, Bold or Angry

♉ **Taurus** – Stable, Reliable or Stubborn

♊ **Gemini** – Talkative, Curious or Nervous

♋ **Cancer** – Maternal, Protective or Moody

♌ **Leo** – Confident, Regal or Demanding

♍ **Virgo** – Organized, Serving or Critical

♎ **Libra** – Balanced, Refined or Indecisive

♏ **Scorpio** – Focused, Intense or Manipulative

♐ **Sagittarius** – International, Outspoken or Privileged

♑ **Capricorn** – Dependable, Serious or Rigid

♒ **Aquarius** – Independent, Eccentric or Detached

♓ **Pisces** – Creative, Mystical or Victim-oriented

THE HOUSES AND THEIR DOMAINS

The planets represent the basic characters or archetypes in the chart. Mars is action and drive, while Venus is about love. All the planets have a different job to do to contribute the whole picture or chart.

1st House — Personality

2nd House — My Money

3rd House — Mind

4th House — Early Home

5th House — Creativity

6th House — Health

7th House — Relationships

8th House — Others' Money

9th House — Higher Education

10th House — Career

11th House — Goals

12th House — Meditation

Ok, now we're going to look at the signature of each planet in the chart of the US. Remember that we're looking at where the planets were in the sky when the Declaration of Independence was signed on July 4th, 1776. The houses that the planets occupy show where each planet expresses itself. Once we get to know the planets, we'll look at the geometry in the middle of the circle or how the planets interact with each other. The thick lines that connect the planets define the gifts and talents of the US. The thin lines represent the challenges of the country. This is the Sacred Geometry or the mandala in the sky. This birth chart defines the purpose of the Unites States.

Notice the group of planets in the 7th house of allies and the 8th house of others' money. The planets clustered there are the Sun, Jupiter and Venus. The Sun, the most important planet in the chart, is located in the 8th house of others' money. The 8th house can be about philanthropy at its best or rampant, unbridled capitalism and debt at its worst. Having Jupiter, the planet of abundance right next to the Sun, gives the promise of great success. But remember that Jupiter is also involved with excess and indulgence, which could result in out-of-control spending. Venus, the planet of beauty is next to them both. Venus likes the best quality and wants to be seen and admired. Yes, Venus can be quite vain. Even though they are all beneficial planets, could it be too much of a good thing? This chart has a definite focus on money and being a showoff. Does the US appear arrogant to the rest of the world?

Now let's see how the planets interact with each other using the angles in the center of the circle. We'll look at the three thin lines or challenges first, then we'll look at the three thick lines or the talents and gifts. Once we get to know those connections, it will be easy to see the purpose of the US. Who is the US – past, present and future?

In the next several charts, I've only included the planets involved in the angle that we're discussing.

Sun Square Saturn: Overindulgence vs Moderation

That first angle to focus on is between the 8th and 11th houses. In the 8th house, the Sun is right next to successful Jupiter and benevolent Venus. This is a fortunate grouping of planets. Used with a positive approach, there is a truly humanitarian intention with these planets, especially in the caring sign of Cancer. The US is here to help humanity and be an international leader in peace, cooperation and philanthropy. But the challenge of Jupiter is lack of moderation. Being in the house of others' money, the US can suffer excessive debt due to overindulgence and overspending. Venus loves luxury and can flaunt it. But the taskmaster, Saturn in the 11th house, is in a challenging angle to them and will make sure they must pay their debts back. Saturn is frugal and not at all prone to indulgence. The taskmaster, Saturn, will see to it that the excess will be dealt with.

The first challenge of the US is overindulgent spending without considering the consequences.

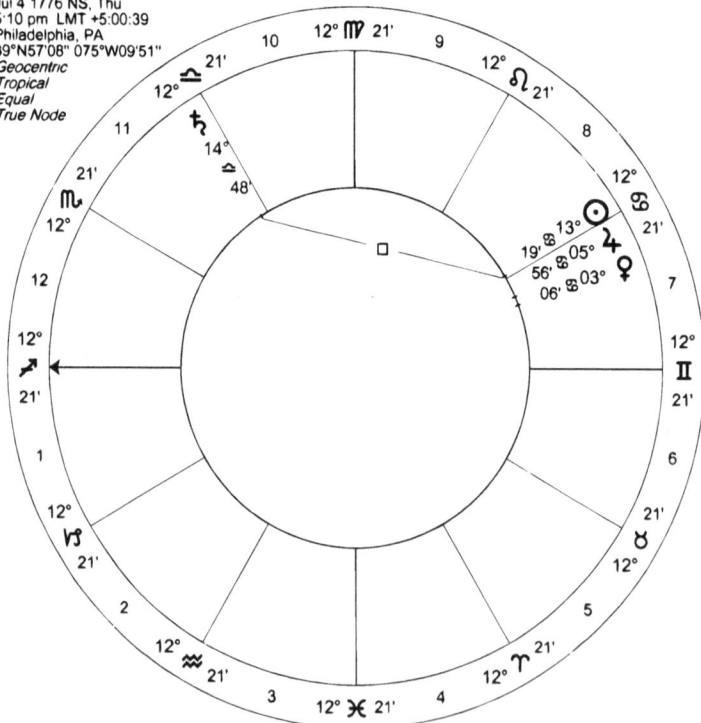

USA Signing Declaration
Natal Chart
Jul 4 1776 NS, Thu
5:10 pm LMT +5:00:39
Philadelphia, PA
39°N57'08" 075°W09'51"
Geocentric
Tropical
Equal
True Node

Pluto Oppose Mercury: Wall Street vs We the People

The second challenging line is from Mercury in the 8th house opposing Pluto in the 2nd house. These are both money houses....my money vs their money (creditors, legal situations, inflation, trade wars, the national economy, the stock market). Mercury in loving Cancer wants to take care of the citizens of the US and help the world. That is in stark contrast to the 2nd house and ruthless Pluto in Capricorn. Capricorn is the sign of business and with Pluto there it is an indication of excessive corporate greed and control of the masses through debt. Is this the new indentured servitude?

The second challenge is striking a financial balance between the corporations and the working class.

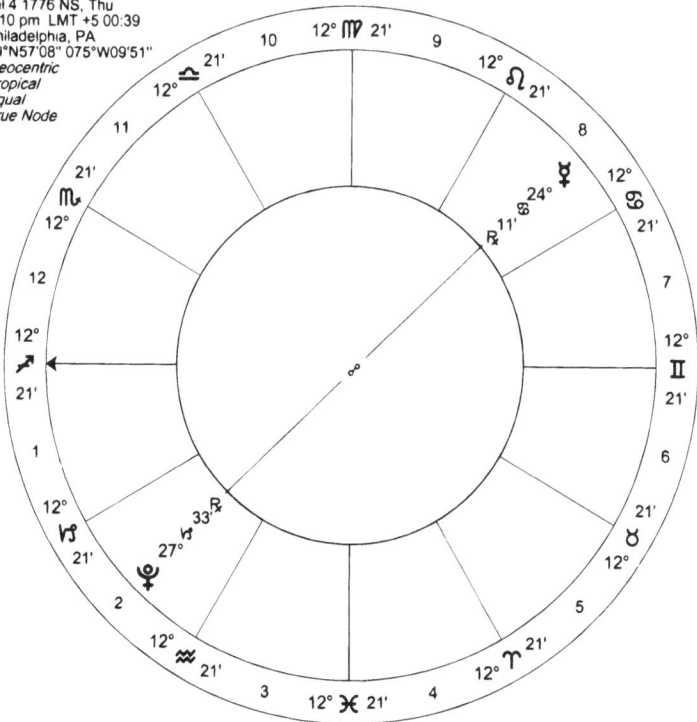

USA Signing Declaration
Natal Chart
Jul 4 1776 NS, Thu
5:10 pm LMT +5 00:39
Philadelphia, PA
39°N57'08" 075°W09'51"
Geocentric
Tropical
Equal
True Node

Neptune Square Mars: Fake News vs the Truth

I've saved the third challenging line for last because it's just so juicy. Slippery Neptune at the top of the chart in the 10th house of reputation challenges aggressive Mars in the 7th house of allies. The negative side of Neptune is involved with deceit, misunderstandings, confusion, underhanded dealings and blatant dishonesty. Events are made confusing on purpose with a challenge to Neptune. Mars is about action but also, military, arms race and the police state. This hard angle adds confusion to the reasoning behind wars or conflicts. How is it that the military industrial complex continues to control the global economy? You can draw your own conclusions. Will the truth ever be told? Maybe not. Neptune is also involved with drugs and alcohol. So, we can include Big Pharma and insurance companies, who both strongarm the American taxpayer.

The last challenge of the US is to be honest regarding the use of military power.

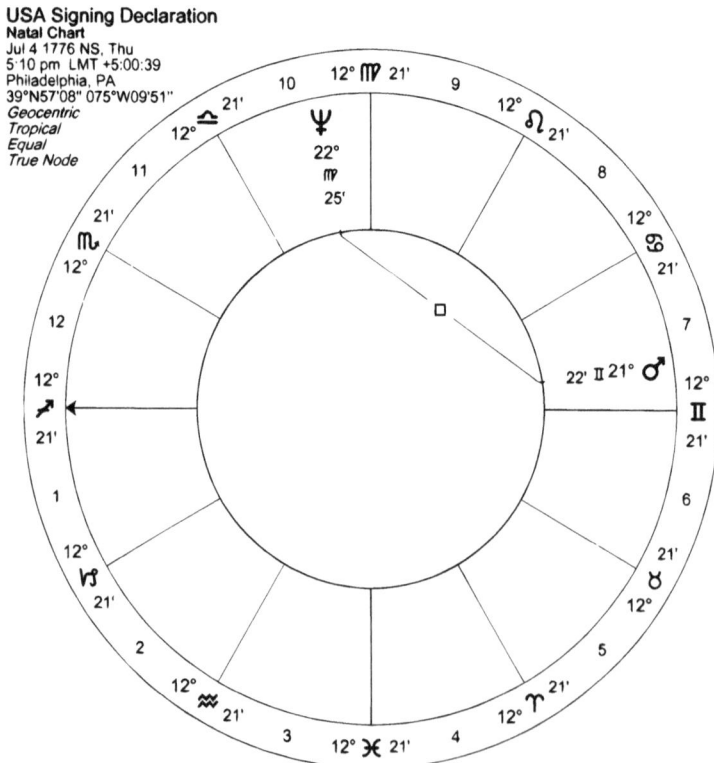

USA Signing Declaration
Natal Chart
Jul 4 1776 NS, Thu
5:10 pm LMT +5:00:39
Philadelphia, PA
39°N57'08" 075°W09'51"
Geocentric
Tropical
Equal
True Node

Now that we have looked at all the challenges in the chart of the US, what do they mean when combined?

In summary of the challenges of the US:

1. Overindulgence.
2. Control of money by the privileged.
3. Aggressive behavior and the lack of transparency.

Now let's look at the positive side of the US. Luckily in Astrology, there are the thick lines or harmonious angles of goodness. There is always a balance of positive and negative in every chart and in every moment in time. It's the astrological Yin and Yang. Never fear, the chart of the US has lots of wonderful angles to balance its challenges.

Saturn Trine Mars and Uranus: Structure of Democracy and Freedom

Most of the positive geometry or thick lines in this chart point toward the right side of the chart, almost like an arrow. The lines from secure Saturn in the 11th house align harmoniously with active Mars and innovative Uranus in intelligent Gemini. These define the ingenuity and new discoveries that the US has typically initiated. Saturn, the planet of business, will make sure that these technologies are successful. In addition, freedom-seeking Uranus joining aggressive Mars speaks to the willingness to fight for independence. This configuration of Saturn, Mars and Uranus is an astrological Declaration of Independence.

The first talent of the US is introducing new concepts to the world and being an example of the ideal of democracy and freedom.

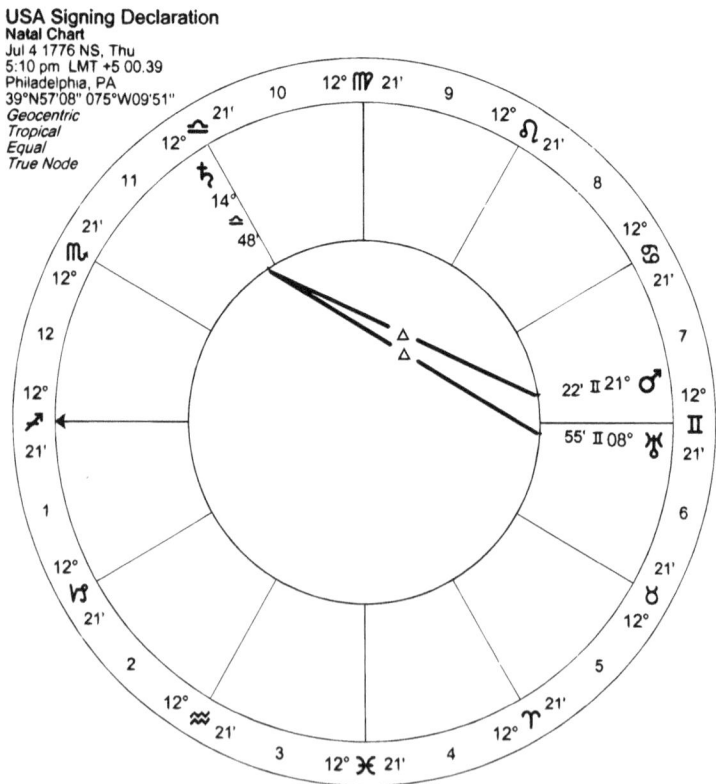

USA Signing Declaration
Natal Chart
Jul 4 1776 NS, Thu
5:10 pm LMT +5 00.39
Philadelphia, PA
39°N57'08" 075°W09'51"
Geocentric
Tropical
Equal
True Node

Moon Trine Mars and Venus: Technologies that Change the World

The other group of positive lines point from the high-tech Aquarius Moon to assertive Mars and receptive Venus. These angles represent the interest in communications and offering original humanitarian ideas to the world. Since the Moon has a finger on the emotional pulse of society, this angle wants to help humanity flourish.

The second talent of the US is contributing new inventions and technologies that will help uplift the world.

USA Signing Declaration
Natal Chart
Jul 4 1776 NS, Thu
5:10 pm LMT +5:00:39
Philadelphia, PA
39°N57'08" 075°W09'51"
Geocentric
Tropical
Equal
True Node

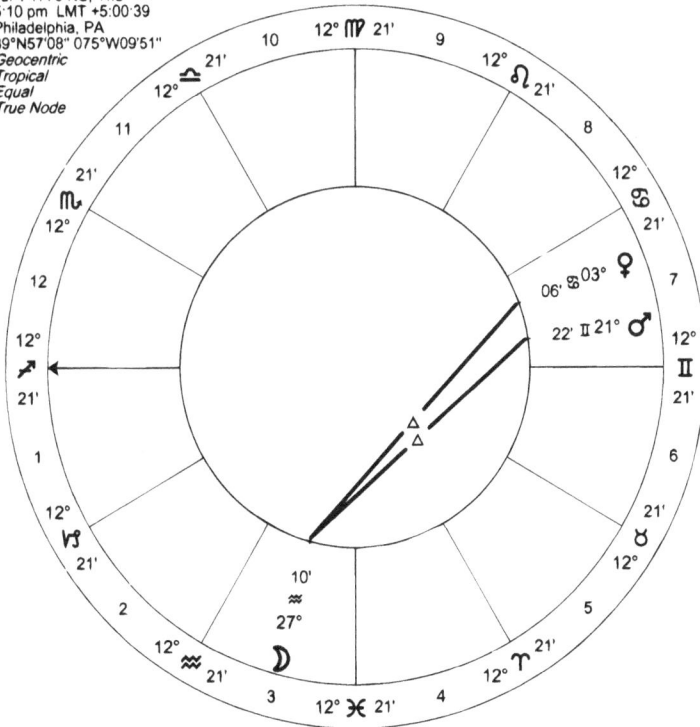

Pluto Trine Neptune: Real Leadership Heals

The last positive line in the chart of the United States is from strongman Pluto in the 2nd house of money to the healer, Neptune, in the 10th house of reputation. Ideally, the US could herald a movement of unity and kindness to help heal and bring the world together in peace. Remember that the controlling side of Pluto is corporate greed. This suggests that Pluto has the opportunity to empower the healer Neptune by using some of that money towards compassionate projects that would enlighten the world. What could be more important at this crucial point in history.

The last talent of the US is being a global leader to help the world heal through compassionate action.

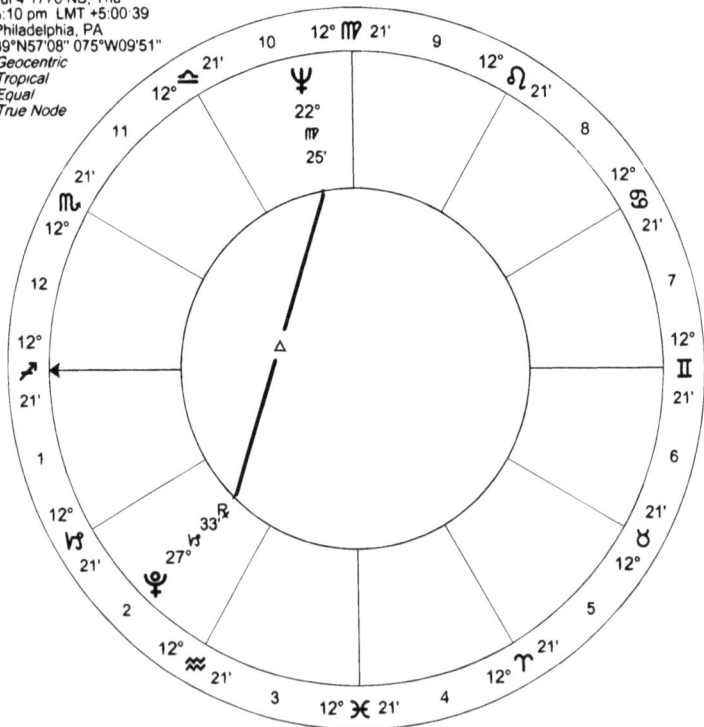

USA Signing Declaration
Natal Chart
Jul 4 1776 NS, Thu
5:10 pm LMT +5:00:39
Philadelphia, PA
39°N57'08" 075°W09'51"
Geocentric
Tropical
Equal
True Node

Now it's time to wrap up the positive side of the US.

In summary of the solid lines or talents of the US:

1. Loving guardianship.
2. Technology, innovation and freewill.
3. Restoring compassion to the world.

The homework of the United States is to work on correcting these three challenges (overindulgence, corporate control of money and aggressive behavior). To fulfill its destiny, the United States must utilize its talents (guardianship, innovation and healing through compassionate acts).

The purpose of the US: to use its leadership, money and strength to help bring the unified world into the future with compassion.

It seems the US in now deciding whether to run with its challenges and control the world or run with its positive lines and help heal the world. Will the US give into the greed and selfishness inherent in this chart or will the US stand up and live its destiny to be an evolved country and help its own citizens and the world?

PART TWO:
What is Happening Now?

Astrology is an accurate clock. The planets in our solar system have exact orbits and can be modeled by computer algorithms for any time in the past or in the future. Astrology uses a technique called Transits. Planetary movements by definition are called Transits. When a transiting planet returns to where it was in the birth chart, events are triggered.

For a person, it can mean anything from getting a promotion at work to having an inner realization that can lead to a major life decision. But in this case, we're doing the chart of the United States so the transits will take on more of a social focus.

Each planet has a different orbit around the Sun. The outer planets have longer orbits. Therefore, they are more significant as a trigger when transiting the birth chart. The more rare the planetary alignment, the more impactful it is.

Planetary Orbits

☽	**Moon**	1 month
☿	**Mercury**	88 days
♀	**Venus**	225 days
♂	**Mars**	687 days or almost 2 years
♃	**Jupiter**	12 years
♄	**Saturn**	30 years
♅	**Uranus**	84 years
♆	**Neptune**	165 years
♇	**Pluto**	249 years

What is happening now? The Pluto Return of the United States . . . let's talk about it.

A planetary return is when a planet makes one revolution around the chart and returns to the same position where it is in the birth chart. If you've had your astrology chart interpreted, you've likely heard about your Saturn return. It happens approximately every 30 years. In contrast, Pluto's orbit is 249 years. It would be impossible for a human being to have a Pluto Return, but a country can have several.

Each planet makes its unique contribution to this clock in the sky. Venus brings love and Mars brings action. Pluto, being the outer most planet, represents death and rebirth at its core. Major transformations occur when Pluto makes a transit in a personal chart. This is when people are born, die, get married or have children . Pluto transits synchronize with all the events that change us forever. The US is just starting its Pluto Return and if it lives up to its reputation it will be an almost total transformation for this country. Is it time for a constitutional convention?

The US is experiencing a pandemic not seen for a century that has caused an economic disaster and is topped off with riots in the streets. These are all perfect examples of the beginning of a Pluto Return. Remember, Pluto can be described with the words Death and Rebirth. The death or elimination of the outdated paradigm must occur first so the rebirth can begin.

Before we get to know this rare and powerful Pluto Return, let's look at three previous Pluto transits or triggers to the chart of the US. The more we learn about Pluto, the better we will understand the current turmoil. To make this easier for you, I've circled Pluto in all these transit charts.

Pluto and WWI

The first Pluto trigger I investigated was the end of WWI, which occurred on November 11, 1918. This led to the beginning of the League of Nations (LON), which was the forerunner to the UN and was created under the Treaty of Versailles. The LON was the first international organization whose purpose was to maintain world peace. Even though Congress never allowed the US to join the League, President Woodrow Wilson was awarded the Nobel Peace Prize for his contribution.

I consider Jupiter and Venus in Cancer one of the best parts of the US chart. As you can see in the chart, Pluto was joining these two benevolent planets when WWI ended. Better international cooperation was the result and was the first time the world ever came together to maintain peace. Pluto always marks a drastic change and this one happened to be a positive transit for the US and for the world. The League of Nations lasted for 26 years but was proven to be helpless against the Axis of Power in the late 1930s. This Pluto transit brought to life some of the best planets in the US chart, which resulted in a fundamental change from the previous 100 years in how countries cooperated with each other.

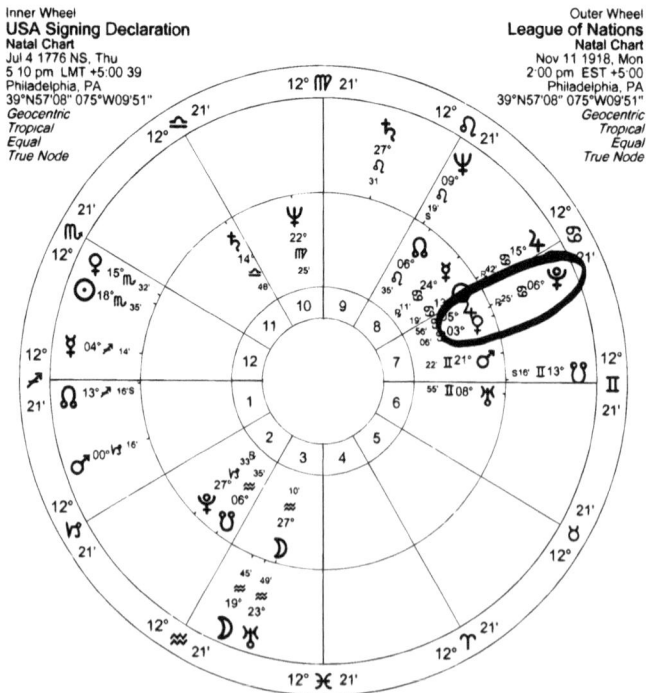

Pluto and Pearl Harbor

The next Pluto event I investigated was Pearl Harbor, which occurred just before 8 a.m. Sunday morning on December 7, 1941. We all know that this was a surprise military attack on the US by the Imperial Japanese Navy. Over the next seven hours there were coordinated attacks on the US military bases in the Philippines, Guam and Wake Island as well as on the British Empire in Malaya, Hong Kong and Singapore. This was virtually the entire Pacific. The very next day, the US was prompted to officially enter WWII.

Pluto can be sneaky. This event was a definite example of the underhanded ruthlessness exhibited by this power planet. The North and South Nodes are points in space that relate to the collective or to the international community. The North Node describes Destiny and the South Node is Karma. In the US chart, Pluto was joining the North Node. Pearl Harbor was an attack on allies who had worked together since WWI, effectively ending the League of Nations. This event realigned the world and which countries trusted each other for collaborating. Pluto always dramatically changes everything it touches.

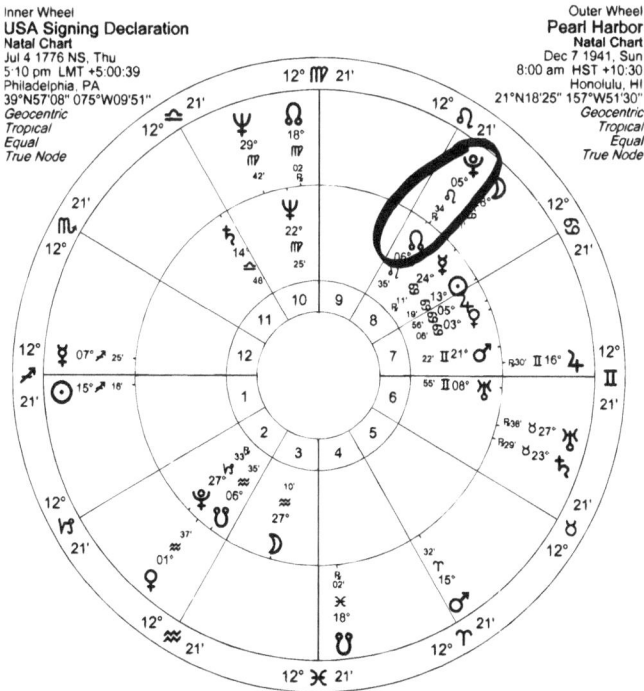

Pluto and 9/11

I consider that the most startling of these three Pluto transits I have chosen to point out to be the attack on the World Trade Center, September 11, 2001. This was another sneak attack that synchronized with a Pluto transit. Look at the chart. Pluto was exactly joining the Rising Sign of the US. Remember I said that the Rising Sign is how the US is perceived by the world. That day Pluto transformed the way the world sees the United States. Because of that tragedy, the US has imposed stricter security measures with the implementation of the Patriot Act and birth of the Department of Homeland Security. The personality of the US as well as how the world perceives it changed radically the morning of 9/11.

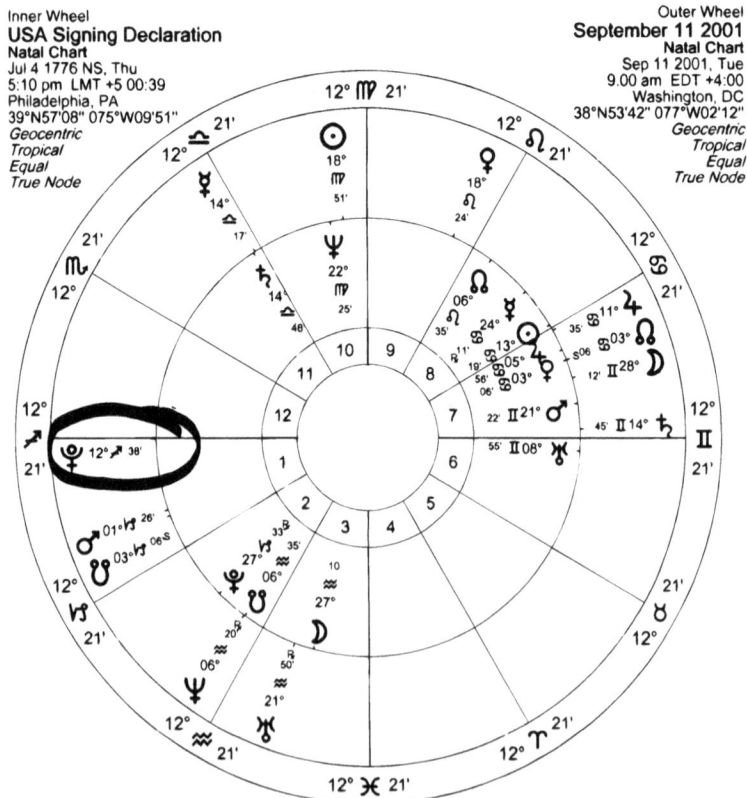

Inner Wheel
USA Signing Declaration
Natal Chart
Jul 4 1776 NS, Thu
5:10 pm LMT +5 00:39
Philadelphia, PA
39°N57'08" 075°W09'51"
Geocentric
Tropical
Equal
True Node

Outer Wheel
September 11 2001
Natal Chart
Sep 11 2001, Tue
9.00 am EDT +4:00
Washington, DC
38°N53'42" 077°W02'12"
Geocentric
Tropical
Equal
True Node

Pluto Return

As you can see, Pluto always triggers changes that affect us at our very core. We looked at WWI, Pearl Harbor and September 11th, which were all perfect examples of events that were triggered by Pluto. Covid-19 with an enormous number of deaths, the US economy in a tailspin and internationally strained relations are now forming a perfect Pluto storm. Enter the Pluto Return!

This is not just a regular Pluto Return – No, No! Instead, Saturn, Jupiter and Pluto are all part of the Pluto Return of the US!

We have a crisis on our hands. Why such a crisis? Let's get to know the planets involved. First, the taskmaster, serious Saturn, is at home in Capricorn so he is much stronger in that sign. It's like having two Saturns. Yikes! But that's what we have now. Saturn has been implementing rules and regulations, like the mandatory lockdown and masks, which he loves to do. Saturn is the hard-nosed executive whose job is to get everyone in line. Jupiter, even though he is normally a beneficial planet, under certain circumstances can show an extremist side. He's like that loud guy at the party who always stirs things up when he drinks too much. Yes, Jupiter likes drama and can do it on an expansive scale. So, instead of helping, Jupiter just turned up the volume and has intensify things. Thanks a lot, Jupiter.

What a team of planets to be with Pluto as he makes his much-anticipated appearance on the scene for his birthday or Pluto Return. He's flanked by Jupiter, the extremist and Saturn, the self-proclaimed boss of the Zodiac. They are a formidable trio who have a mission to change things drastically and with a dramatic flair.

This is beyond rare. This configuration has never happened before and will never happen again. The next Pluto Return in 249 years will not include Saturn and Jupiter. This is so unusual that it will absolutely cause immense, radical and historic changes to this country. Remember that the Pluto Return is occurring in the US house of money. We have the Covid virus, we're on lockdown and we have an economy that is teetering on the brink of disaster.

The Pluto Return is triggering off the opposition to Mercury in the chart.

That angle is about corporate greed versus the needs of the people and the Earth, itself. *Do we need to find a new type of economy that honors the Earth rather than greedily plundering the resources to keep the economy alive?*

Pluto wants to change things from the inside out and with the current spotlight on the White House, that appears to be happening. Government, financial institutions, the retail industry, hospitality, travel, medicine, global allies are all entities that are currently in crisis. Pluto will expose what is broken. Saturn will inspect the damage and it looks to me like Jupiter could turn it into a fiasco. The world will never be the same after this Pluto Return. This has already begun and won't be completed until 2024 or 2025. We are in for a few action-packed years before the new paradigm emerges.

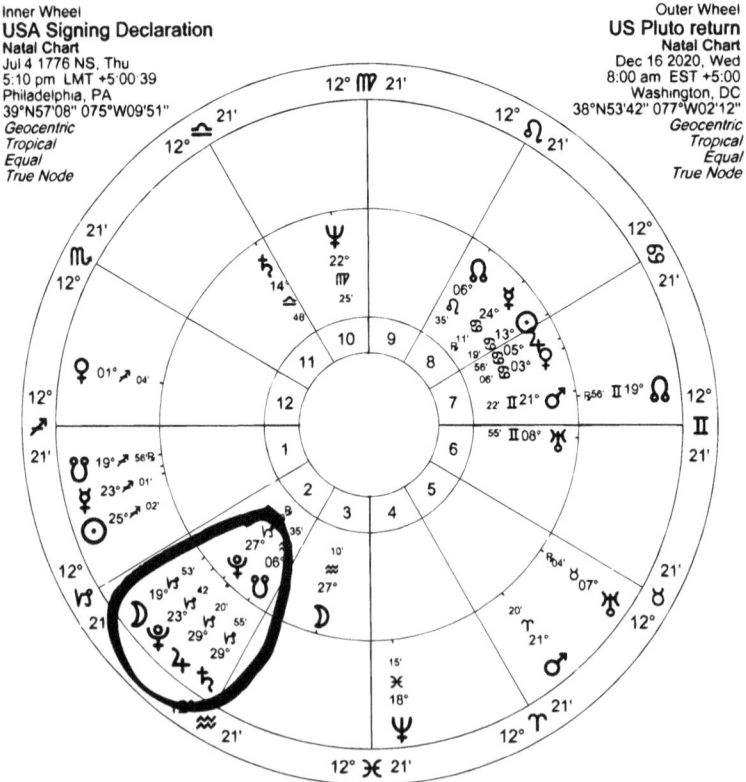

Inner Wheel
USA Signing Declaration
Natal Chart
Jul 4 1776 NS, Thu
5:10 pm LMT +5:00 39
Philadelphia, PA
39°N57'08" 075°W09'51"
Geocentric
Tropical
Equal
True Node

Outer Wheel
US Pluto return
Natal Chart
Dec 16 2020, Wed
8:00 am EST +5:00
Washington, DC
38°N53'42" 077°W02'12"
Geocentric
Tropical
Equal
True Node

PART THREE:
The Astrological Ages

Before we look at the future of the United States, let's travel into the distant past. One of the largest cycles in Astrology is the change of an Astrological Age, which happens approximately every 2,150 years. The Age of Pisces started around the birth of Christ. We're now leaving the Age of Pisces and entering the Age of Aquarius and the transition is causing great confusion. Now I'll explain how the Ages change. The mechanism is called the **Precession of the Equinoxes** and this is how it works.

The Earth isn't a perfect sphere and has a bulge around the Equator. That bulge, with the gravitational pull of the Moon, give the Earth a wobble. If you visualize a spinning top, the peak or axis will do a circular rotation as the top spins. The same thing happens to the Earth. One complete rotation of this axis is called a Great Year and takes approximately 25,800 years.

As that occurs, the Spring Equinox will move backward through the 12 signs of the Zodiac and will take about 2,150 years to go through each sign. Because it goes backward, it's called the Precession of the Equinoxes. If it went forward, it would be called the Procession of the Equinoxes. The change of an astrological age coincides with major shifts in culture and society, so I was curious and wanted to look back and see some previous Ages to prepare us for our current transition from the Age of Pisces to Aquarius.

The Age of Cancer (8,640 BC – 6,480 BC)

Matriarchy, Food, Agriculture, Nurturing, Settled Communities and Family.

The Age of the Great Mother

The sign of Cancer is associated with the Moon and the act of childbearing, caring and protecting the family. The Neolithic Revolution from 9,000 – 6,000 BC marked the beginning of civilization. This is the age that first saw permanent housing which marked the domestication of humanity as well as animals. This replaced the previous nomadic tribes of hunters and gatherers who constantly traveled to follow herds of animals in pursuit of food.

Spiritually, this was the peak of the matriarchal culture and included worshipping the Goddess. Figurines and sculptures of full-figured Mother Goddesses were found by archeologists all over the world from this era.

The Age of Gemini (6,480 BC – 4,320 BC)

Written Communication, Language, Learning, Manual Dexterity, Travel and Trade.

The Age of Communication and Trade

The sign of Gemini is associated with Mercury and language, thinking, learning and travel. This was the first industrial age. Humanity saw the beginning of craft industries, movement and trade. Extensive trade routes were built that linked the Mediterranean Sea with southern Russia. The main commodity during this era was the exchange of craft techniques and ideas rather than the actual crafts themselves. At the beginning of this age, ceramics were plain but within a couple of centuries developed into being decorated and using glazes. The art was symbolic and included shapes like crosses and chevrons that evolved into mythological and religious symbols. Later they evolved into alphabets as well written languages. The Proto-Indo-European language was developed around 5,000 BC and is the basis of most modern languages.

Spiritually, this was the era of multiple gods as in the Greek pantheon of gods and goddesses, like Zeus, Demeter, Apollo and Aphrodite. Hermes, or Mercury in Roman lore, is associated with travel, communications, borders, diplomacy and eloquence. Mercury relates to Gemini.

The Age of Taurus (4,320 – 2,160 BC)

Wealth, comfort, banking, refinement, peace and the building of monuments.

The Age of the Earth, Agriculture and the Bull

The sign of Taurus is associated with Venus and finances, comforts, refinements and monuments. Money and banking were invented during this era. The earliest examples of writing were lists used by religion and business to note the exchange of goods and real estate. Towns were built as marketplaces and therefore became wealthy. Money and refinement became the measure of growth during the Age of Taurus.

This is approximately the time of the building of the Great Pyramids in Egypt as well as huge monuments in Mesoamerica. Pyramid-shaped ziggurats used for observing the sky as well as an attempt to get closer to their spiritual source, were also constructed during this age. Rulers and Pharaohs were buried in megalithic tombs with all their gold treasures to be enjoyed in the afterlife. How perfectly Taurus.

Spiritually, organized religion emerged with the Taurus symbol of the bull-god as their focus of worship and chief deity. Bull worshipping cults began in Assyria, Egypt and Crete during this era. Religions were closely tied to the collection of wealth. The pharaoh in Egypt as well as in Mesopotamia, collected and distributed all the wealth in the country.

The Age of Aries (2,160 BC – 1 AD)

Competition, Anger, Aggression, Heroes, Weapons and Warfare.

The Age of War, Fire and the Ram

The sign of Aries is associated with Mars and action, courage and conquering, often with aggression. The relative peaceful Age of Taurus transitioned to an age of war. The smelting of iron replaced the soft and dull swords made of bronze during the previous age. This is when the first military empires began that lead to rampant invading and conquering.

Alexander the Great's world empire opened the door for the Roman Empire. In China, the aggressive Shang Dynasty conquered peaceful farming communities and created the first military dynasty. The same trend occurred in Mexico with the Olmecs with statues of heads wearing helmets either for war or for sports.

Spiritually, there was a drive to replace the polytheistic belief of multiple gods with the monotheistic dogma of one supreme being. Hero myths where a single warrior wins his way to glory was the dominant belief as the perfect male body like Hercules, Spartacus and Moses were revered.

During the Age of Aries, masculine gods fought the established feminine goddesses and by all appearances won. This marked the change from matriarchy to patriarchy. Even the new style of the supreme being is quick to anger and punish those who questioned his authority. He is pictured as a general with his chosen people or army fighting and wiping out the previous believers, now considered to be pagans. Does that sound like Mars to you?

The Age of Pisces (1 AD – 2,150 AD)

Religion, Spirituality, Prophecies and Prophets, Illusion, Addictions and Fear.

The Age of religion, spirituality, and illusion

The sign of Pisces is associated with Neptune and transcendence, prophesies, dreams, insecurity and submission. This has been the age of major world religions such as Christianity, Judaism, Islam, Buddhism, Hinduism that has dominated the geopolitical landscape. Enlightenment became the focus. The hero-warrior morphed into the saint, prophet, sage and guru. The Christians claimed Jesus as their ultimate prophet and the Muslims saw Muhammed as theirs. The core of these religions, especially Christianity, is prophecy and predicting the ending times. The Age of Pisces also produced exquisite art, music as well as advancement in the sciences during the Renaissance. Prophecy indicates that there will be a spiritual battle between good and evil, Heaven and Hell or between God and Satan, that will herald the beginning of the golden Age of Aquarius.

Spiritually, organized religion based on the predictions of prophets came into power. Many countries became theocracies where government and church were the same. Monotheistic beliefs were imposed making it a sin to worship more than one God. The Crusades and the Spanish Inquisition enforced over-zealous religious practices, making submission to these ideas a law. The Age of Pisces is perfectly defined by humanity giving its power away to a perceived external illusion of salvation or, eternal damnation.

The Age of Aquarius (2,150 AD – 4,300 AD)

Technology, Individuality, Global Connectivity, Ecology, Inventions and Liberty

The Age of Reason and Science

The sign of Aquarius is associated with Uranus and new inventions, technology, independence, equality, individuality, the environment and being globally connected. Humanity will be linked through computers and the internet, but there will be a deeper connectedness. The world will be forced to work as one due to the climate changes we are now facing. But another side of Aquarius is people thinking independently and refusing to be controlled by authority figures. A perfect example of Aquarius is the internet, where everyone is independent yet unified under the matrix of social media. The planet associated with Aquarius is Uranus, the Rebel, who demands nothing less than a paradigm shift. Therefore, the qualities of independence, freedom, innovation and personal creativity are at the core of this Age.

Spiritually, this Age will bring an independence of thought and beliefs that will challenge the older Piscean religious dogmas that were based on submission to a higher being. Humanity will experience that the power lies within and not through an outdated hierarchy of an in-between man or priest who talks to God for you. In the Age of Aquarius, everyone will connect to their own source personally.

PART FOUR:
The Future

After a fascinating jaunt through the Astrological Ages, let's see what the beginning of the Aquarian Age might look like. There is a lot of discussion as to when the Aquarian Age will actually start. Some say that it began in 1945 with the atomic age. Others feel the 1960s were the beginning with peace, love, unity and the Dawning of the Age of Aquarius. The musical, Hair, was a great introduction.

For this book, I used the dates calculated by Neil Mann, who puts the ingress year or the very beginning of the Aquarian Age at 2,150 AD and lasting until 4,300 AD! Regardless of the exact birth date of this age, we are experiencing the ending of Pisces and the beginning of Aquarius in the world now. It feels like we're all in the birth canal and the squeeze is real. With our journey through the Ages, we now know how unique one Age is from the next, and the Aquarian Age will be no different. Bye Pisces —- Hi Aquarius!

What is Aquarius all about? It is the sign of new inventions, technology, freedom, equality, the environment, and a collective consciousness. Aquarius is not known for being subtle, so we can expect a dramatic beginning to this dynamic age of freedom and independence. It is starting with global protests demanding a new way of living which is fueled by the internet and social media. It should be a great awakening. Uniting humanity will become important. Communal living will be more common.

The sign of Aquarius has a definite independent and aloof quality, which sure can be seen in this era of masks and social distancing. Since the world has been on lockdown with the Covid-19 virus, what has been happening? Yes, everyone is stuck inside their home, but what are they doing? Anything Aquarian? Well, thank goodness for the internet, because that has been our common ground. The new phrase is "We're all in this together". Entertainment is being streamed into people's homes instead of everyone traveling to go to concerts, theatre or sporting events. Many are working remotely from their laptops at home instead of driving the freeway to work at a huge, corporate compound. Office buildings, malls and stadiums might be the dinosaurs from the end of the Age of Pisces. Maybe they will become campuses for the homeless.

Out of necessity, an incredible number of people are deciding to become entrepreneurs instead of working for someone else, which will avoid the possibility of getting fired again. That fact alone will stimulate inventions that will soon become mainstream. Aquarius is very innovative. Old habits are being broken. As a result of everyone staying home, the Earth has gotten a break from human activity and has done an incredible job of healing herself in a very short period of time. The skies and the water are much cleaner and there is an eerie calm. In an odd way, the world is much smaller and more connected than it was a few months ago. Because of home schooling due to the virus, free computers and Wi-fi are being given to underprivileged children to help balance socio-economic equality.

This is all quintessentially Aquarius.

The US is entering the most dramatic time of change since its birth in 1776 because of this Pluto Return. This is a total transformation for the country. We can see the change has already started and will continue for the next few years at least. The Pluto Return is not even complete until 2024 AD. It won't be easy, but it's necessary for the United States to become an adult. Pluto will see to it.

Another side of Aquarius is independence and equality, which is the core of the Declaration of Independence, the Constitution and the Bill of Rights. The writers and founders of the Constitution were visionaries. They innately understood that the best contribution of the United States would be to usher in the Age of Aquarius, through the concept of Democracy. "We the People" is definitely Aquarian.

I wanted to refresh my memory and look at the defining creeds of the United States to discover their Aquarian ideals: The Declaration of Independence, the Constitution and the Bill of Rights.

This Declaration of Independence was a document that cut our political ties, so the US was no longer under British rule. It was signed on July 4, 1776 and is celebrated each year as our national holiday of independence. Here is the famous statement of individual rights. "We hold these truths to be self-evident, that all men are created equal that they are endowed by their creator with certain unalienable rights, that among these are life, liberty and the pursuit of happiness. (Does that mean only white men? That's very Piscean. What about women and ethnicities?)

The Constitution is the supreme law of the United States of America. It defines the national structure of government and has three parts: The Preamble, the Bill of Rights and the Amendments.

The Preamble
We the People of the United States, in order to form a more perfect Union, establish justice, insure domestic tranquility, provide for the common defense, promote the general welfare, and secure the blessings of liberty to ourselves and our posterity, do ordain and establish this Constitution for the United States of America.

The Bill of Rights
The first 10 amendments are collectively known as the Bill of Rights. These amendments explain the rights of American citizens in relation to the government. It guarantees personal and civil rights to everyone – like freedom of speech, press and religion. It defines the separation of power between the three branches of the government: Legislative (Congress), Executive (President) and Judicial (Supreme Court and other Federal Courts). It also states the rules for due process of law and dictates that all powers not delegated to the Federal Government be given to the people or to the states.

1st Amendment — Protects freedom of speech, the press and the right to assemble to protest the government to fix problems.

2nd Amendment — Gives citizens the right to keep and bear arms.

3rd Amendment — Prevents the government from forcing homeowners to allow soldiers to use their homes. Before the American Revolution, British soldiers could confiscate private homes.

4th Amendment — Protects citizens from unreasonable search and seizure without a warrant on an individual or their private property. Warrants must be issued by a judge and based on probable cause.

5th Amendment — Protects citizens from prosecution without due process, being tried twice for the same offense and self-incrimination (the right to remain silent by Taking the Fifth). People cannot be imprisoned without due process of law.

6th Amendment — Assures the right of an individual to a speedy and public trial by a jury and to the right to be represented by a lawyer.

7th Amendment — Extends the rights to a jury trial in Federal civil cases.

8th Amendment — Prohibits excessive bail and fines, and cruel and unusual punishments.

9th Amendment — Explains that listing specific rights in the Constitution does not exclude other rights that have not been defined.

10th Amendment — Reveals that the Federal Government only has those powers delegated in the Constitution. If the power is not listed, it belongs to the states or to the people.

The Amendments
Most of the later amendments expand individual civil rights protections. Other amendments modify the procedures of the government.

Now that we've had a crash course in high school civics, it's obvious that the founders of the US Constitution were visionaries and understood the Aquarian concept of personal freedoms. In fact, even though Benjamin Franklin is best known for being an inventor and discovering electricity, he was also an excellent astrologer. It's documented that he used astrology to select the date to sign the Declaration of Independence. He was a

Freemason and was the founder of the Masonic Lodge in the colonies. George Washington was also a Mason as were 35 of his generals and nine signers of the Declaration of Independence. It is said that George Washington took his oath of office with a Bible he borrowed from the New York Masonic Lodge. The essence of Freemasonry, which was quite popular then, was the promotion of brotherly love. All this comes back to Aquarius! Remember the keywords for Aquarius are freedom, equality, brotherhood and collective consciousness.

In summary...

We've gotten to know the astrology chart of the United States. The challenges for the US are overindulgence, money controlled by the privileged and the lack of transparency with aggressive behaviors. Luckily, the talents of the US are quite spectacular, which are loving guardianship, innovation and compassion. The destiny of the US is to use its strengths to help bring the world into the future with compassion.

We've also learned that the US is just starting to experience its rare and life-changing Pluto Return. Remember that I chose three previous Pluto events. They were the end of WWI, Pearl Harbor and 9/11. Since this Pluto Return involves the excessive Jupiter and stern Saturn, it will be memorable and undoubtably more intense than any of the previous Pluto triggers.

We traveled back through several Astrological Ages, starting at almost 9,000 BC. That journey allowed us to see how unique each age is.

Since our topic is the future of the United States, we got to know civics and the Constitution, the Declaration of Independence and the Bill of Rights. I found that the vision of the founding fathers was very Aquarian.

After all this research, what is my conclusion? First, the United States needs to reinvent itself during this Pluto Return. The next few years will tell us if the US is becoming the best version of itself and will grow into its destiny as the humanitarian leader of the world. Or will it try to strongarm the world with its military machine and greed? I'm hoping that We the People will demand, through our votes and our collective consciousness, that the US will become the best version of itself and will lead the world into the Aquarian Age.

If the US is as Aquarian as I am presenting here, its future will depend on We the People. After this death and rebirth, thanks to the Pluto Return, a new America will emerge that will embody the intended purpose of the constitution... one of unity, equality and compassion.

Davos, the annual World Economic Forum in Switzerland, is a perfect example of the Aquarian ideal. Leaders and influencers of the world come together to discuss strategies to implement new ways to confront the Earth's greatest issues. The Aquarian Age is the Age of Technology. We are now witnessing technology's great influence over the planet with 2,666 satellites, and counting, currently orbiting the Earth. Let's face it, after all that we've been through in 2020, it's time for a reboot. Could this be the Great Reset?

Another Aquarian style is always striving for a better future and growth, which is seen in "We the People of the United States, in order to form a more perfect Union...". The United States isn't perfect but will always strive to become more perfect.

Is it the time for another Constitutional Convention?

It is time to abolish the Electoral College?

My intention is for this book to be a message of hope and empowerment.

You and I are **We the People**.

We each have a necessary voice and as a unified people, together we will create the Future of the United States.

www.ingramcontent.com/pod-product-compliance
Lightning Source LLC
Chambersburg PA
CBHW060542030426
42337CB00021B/4400